The Lightnings of God

Warren Hunter

Sword Ministries International
Branson, Missouri

The Lightnings of God
Published by:
Sword Ministries International
FMB 649
3044 Shepherd of the Hills
Exprwy No. 100
Branson, MO 65616
ISBN 1-889816-19-1

Cover design & Book production by:
DB & Associates Design Group, Inc.
dba Double Blessings Productions
P.O. Box 52756, Tulsa, OK 74152
www.doubleblessing.com

Printed in the United States of America.

Contents

"The LORD thundered from heaven, and the Most High uttered His voice.

He sent out arrows and scattered them; lightning bolts, and He vanquished them."

— *2 Samuel 22:14,15*

Contents

Introduction

I have always been fascinated with the power of God. In my search and hunger for Him, the Lord began reminding me of places in the natural where I have seen great power like volcanoes, thunder, and lightning. When I was thirteen years old, I would go camping with my friends. During those days, we didn't pitch a tent; we just laid in our sleeping bags around a campfire and watched the stars until we fell asleep. I remember one night while sleeping, a thunderous rain broke out and lightning struck different places in the mountains where we were camping. We covered ourselves in our sleeping bags and enjoyed God's weather show. The next day we discovered a place where lightning had struck and made a large hole in the ground. The tree it struck was burned up!

While ministering on the subject of the supernatural many years later, the Lord led me into a study of how lightning works in the natural. As I dug deeper into the subject, the Lord began showing me the supernatural side of His spiritual lightning strikes that burn and conduit through man's being!

Get ready! You are about to experience powerful revelation that will prepare you to experience the lightning of God.

Chapter 1
Understanding High Places

Once while ministering in a crusade and as I prayed for this man the lightning of God struck him through his chest. He had cancer in both lungs and was totally bald. I saw this man months later he had blond curly hair and was totally healed. He was sixty-seven years old. His hair grew back curly. The lightning curled his hair.

Before we can understand lightning power flowing through us, we must understand the high places. As we expound throughout the book, you will come to understand the importance of high places and contact points in relationship to power.

The sinners in Zion are afraid; Fearfulness has seized the hypocrites: "Who among us shall dwell with the devouring fire? Who among us shall dwell with everlasting burnings?"

He who walks righteously and speaks uprightly, he who despises the gain of oppressions, who gestures with his hands, refusing bribes, who stops his ears from hearing of bloodshed, and shuts his eyes from seeing evil:

He will dwell on high; his place of defense will be the fortress of rocks; bread will be given him, his water will be sure.

Isaiah 33:14-16

1

Strongholds in High Places

In the above verse, we see there is strength from dwelling consumed in God presence. God wants His strength to grow to the point that power releases His lightning through you, but power will not be released if you don't tear down the high places in your life. The spiritual high places in people's lives are strongholds within us that are either consecrated to God...or to Satan. *Whatever you meditate upon will take dominion over you and it will establish a stronghold in your mind.* If you meditate upon the Word of God, it will become your stronghold, and that is the kind of stronghold you need. If you meditate upon trash, a stronghold of trash will be built in your mind and your heart. In America, we think that because we have the Word we have the liberty to participate in whatever we want. Paul said, "Can I sin that grace may abound? God forbid!"

When the Israelites came into the land of Canaan, they were ordered to destroy the high places of the people who lived in the land, because they were worshipping false gods in the high places. We get offended if someone starts attacking the evil high places in our lives. Our high places are where compromise takes place, and God hates it. Compromise breeds lack of stability in Christians.

"For the children of Judah have done evil in My sight," says the LORD. "They have set their abominations in the house which is called by My name, to pollute it.

"And they have built the *high places of Tophet*, which is in the Valley of the Son of Hinnom, to burn their sons and their daughters in the fire,

which I did not command, nor did it come into My heart.   **Jeremiah 7:30,31**

Idols in High Places

What are they doing? They are building idols on the high places. The nations began to offer sacrifices upon the high places. Modern readers of the Old Testament often miss the significance of Canaanite idolatry. The worship of a Canaanite god or goddess was no minor blemish in Israel's history. Besides having a devastatingly debasing effect on the practitioner, the acts of worship were fundamentally opposed to the worship of the living God.[1]

What were they doing in these "high places of Tophet?" I looked up the word "Tophet" and it is interesting what it means.[2] "Tophet"or "Topheth", the most probable is its connection with a root meaning "burning" — the "place of burning." Strong's Concordance defines the word as smiting or contempt. Israel offered sacrifices that were contemptible to God upon the high places. When they began to intermarry with the other nations they began to worship their gods. One of the false gods they worshipped was called Asherah, the pagan goddess of fertility. She was depicted upon a carved wooden pole. A stone pillar depicted the male deity Baal. Incense was burned and the sacrifice of animals and children was practiced on these high places. They would also pray and eat sacrificial meals.

and had walked in the statutes of the nations whom the LORD had cast out from before the children of Israel, and of the kings of Israel, which they had made.

Also the children of Israel secretly did against the LORD their God things that were not right,

and they built for themselves high places in all their cities, from watchtower to fortified city.

They set up for themselves sacred pillars and wooden images on every high hill and under every green tree.

There they burned incense on all the high places, like the nations whom the LORD had carried away before them; and they did wicked things to provoke the LORD to anger,

for they served idols, of which the LORD had said to them, "You shall not do this thing."

2 Kings 17:8-12

Today Maypoles are celebrated every May 1 in Norway and Sweden. They almost certainly have their origin in phallic shrine, which orgiastic worshippers danced around her in celebration of the male sex organ. Asherah is the name of a Canaanite goddess of sex and war. This was a vivid representation of paganism in its most corrupt manifestations, and could be compared to today's modern pornography.

Break down their altars, smash their sacred stones and cut down their Asherah poles.

Do not worship any other god, for the LORD, whose name is Jealous, is a jealous God.

Exodus 34:13,14 (NIV)

They also set up for themselves high places, sacred stones and Asherah poles on every high hill and under every spreading tree.

1 King 14:23 (NIV)

Understanding the history and contemporary significance of these high places is important, because before we can understand the lightning of God, we must choose whose high place we will dwell in — God's, or Satan's. The high place is a contact point. An evil high place in your life is anything that exalts itself against God. And this is where our battle rests.

For we do not wrestle against flesh and blood, but against principalities, against powers, against the rulers of the darkness of this age, against spiritual hosts of wickedness in the heavenly places.

Ephesians 6:12

High places are places of moral temptation. This is why God commanded them to be destroyed. When they did not destroy them, they began to worship their false gods and accept their immoral behavior. If you don't deal with the altars on the high places then you will be accepting immoral behavior.

Chapter 2
The High Place of "Religion"

The Israelites were to worship God in a tabernacle called Shiloh. Shiloh means "tranquil." Shiloh was set up in the high places as an epithet or symbol of the Messiah. This is why Jesus would go up to the mountain in the nighttime to pray. It was very important for Him to make contact with God in the high places. These were great places of intimacy with His Father.

When the children of Israel came together in unity to worship God in the high places, God would subdue their enemies under them.

Now the whole congregation of the children of Israel assembled together at Shiloh, and set up the tabernacle of meeting there. And the land was subdued before them.
Joshua 18:1

There are only two kings mentioned in the Old Testament who dealt with the high places: Hezekiah and Josiah. Hezekiah destroyed Israel's high place of "religion" where Moses' infamous brazen serpent was placed by the people for worship upon a pole and brought revival to the land.

Now it came to pass in the third year of Hoshea the son of Elah, king of Israel, that Hezekiah the son of Ahaz, king of Judah, began to reign.

He was twenty-five years old when he became king, and he reigned twenty-nine years in Jerusalem. His mother's name was Abi the daughter of Zechariah.

And he did what was right in the sight of the LORD, according to all that his father David had done.

He removed the high places and broke the sacred pillars, cut down the wooden image and broke in pieces the bronze serpent that Moses had made; for until those days the children of Israel burned incense to it, and called it Nehushtan.

2 Kings 18:1-4

This correlates with Colossians 2:8, which speaks of the religious high places of traditions, philosophies and ideas of men. Colossians 2:8 identifies what stops you from receiving Colossians 2:9-10.

See to it that no one carries you off as spoil or makes you captive by so called philosophy and intellectualism and vain deceit, plain nonsense, fancies following human traditions, mans ideas and thoughts of material rather than the spiritual world. Just crude notions following the rudimentary elementary regarding the teachings of Christ the Messiah.

For in Him the whole fullness of Diety (the Godhead) continues to dwell in bodily form [giving complete expression of the divine nature]

And you are in Him, made full and having come to fullness of life [in Christ you too are filled with the Godhead — Father, Son and Holy Spirit- and reach full spiritual stature]. And He is the

8

head of all rule and authority [of every angelic principality and power].

Colossians 2:8-10 (AMP)

Religious Strongholds Bring Division

Nothing will stop the lightning of God from exploding in the church faster than the high place of religion. Those given to such vain traditions never experience the fullness of the Godhead Paul describes in verses 9 and 10.

Think about it. Every time there is a reaction in the church on something religious there is division. A new denomination rises up. This is a religious stronghold. The new denomination rises up because we don't know how to deal with the religious strongholds when they rise up. So, we have a new denomination. Then we wonder why the power of God doesn't flow.

For example, there are now seven or eight different branches of the Church of God, many different Charismatic Word of Faith groups, even several Baptist, Methodist, Luthern, etc. There is a new denomination started every year because of religious strongholds. Division produces strife, and the power doesn't flow. It is very important what the children of Israel did with the high places. They followed cultural religious practices of the nations surrounding Israel rather than keeping the covenant stipulated by God. It is very important that you keep covenant with God. The kingdom of God has come and it is within us. We are sanctified and set apart to be the dwelling place of God. We are called to be the Holy of Holies. We are called to be God's high place upon the earth. That is what He intends for us. You are the lightning rod and you need to get a revelation of that.

[He planned] for the maturity of the times and the climax of the ages to unify all things and head

them up and consummate them in Christ [both]
things in heaven and things on earth.

Ephesians 1:10 (AMP)

Who Occupies the High Place in Your Life?

If you want to experience the lightning of God's revival, you will need to eliminate every high thing in your life that isn't consecrated to God. Like Josiah who destroyed the altars on the high places brought revival to the land of Judah in 2 Kings 23, you must do some idol smashing too. Then you must worship God only, as Hezekiah did. King Hezekiah restored Judah's temple, reappointed the priesthood and re-established the Passover (see 2 Chronicles 29, 30).

Hezekiah and Josiah had the courage to destroy the high places in Judah. If you want God's high place to reign in your life, allow these good king's actions to speak to your life.

And the king commanded Hilkiah the high priest, the priests of the second order, and the doorkeepers, to bring out of the temple of the LORD all the articles that were made for Baal, for Asherah, and for all the host of heaven; and he burned them outside Jerusalem in the fields of Kidron, and carried their ashes to Bethel.

Then he removed the idolatrous priests whom the kings of Judah had ordained to burn incense on the high places in the cities of Judah and in the places all around Jerusalem, and those who burned incense to Baal, to the sun, to the moon, to the constellations, and to all the host of heaven.

And he brought out the wooden image from the house of the LORD, to the Brook Kidron outside Jerusalem, burned it at the Brook Kidron and ground it to ashes, and threw its ashes on the graves of the common people.

Then he tore down the ritual booths of the perverted persons that were in the house of the LORD, where the women wove hangings for the wooden image.

And he brought all the priests from the cities of Judah, and defiled the high places where the priests had burned incense, from Geba to Beersheba; also he broke down the high places at the gates which were at the entrance of the Gate of Joshua the governor of the city, which were to the left of the city gate.

Nevertheless the priests of the high places did not come up to the altar of the LORD in Jerusalem, but they ate unleavened bread among their brethren.

And he defiled Topheth, which is in the Valley of the Son of Hinnom, that no man might make his son or his daughter pass through the fire to Molech.

Then he removed the horses that the kings of Judah had dedicated to the sun, at the entrance to the house of the LORD, by the chamber of Nathan-Melech, the officer who was in the court; and he burned the chariots of the sun with fire.

The altars that were on the roof, the upper chamber of Ahaz, which the kings of Judah had made, and the altars which Manasseh had made in the two courts of the house of the LORD, the king broke down and pulverized there, and threw their dust into the Brook Kidron.

Then the king defiled the high places that were east of Jerusalem, which were on the south of the Mount of Corruption, which Solomon king of Israel had built for Ashtoreth the abomination of the Sidonians, for Chemosh the abomination of the Moabites, and for Milcom the abomination of the people of Ammon.

And he broke in pieces the sacred pillars and cut down the wooden images, and filled their places with the bones of men.

Moreover the altar that was at Bethel, and the high place which Jeroboam the son of Nebat, who made Israel sin, had made, both that altar and the high place he broke down; and he burned the high place and crushed it to powder, and burned the wooden image.

2 Kings 23:4-15

Today we sit in the body of Christ with limited power because the high places in our Christian culture have not been dealt with. There is no shortage of power. It simply won't flow from on high if the high places aren't dealt with. Remember, whoever rules the high places causes a flow or stops the power. When the lightning strikes there can only be one target and then all the fullness of the power will flow. When there is a multitude of targets on the mountain then the lightning will be displaced and power will be diverted. You won't experience all the power that you are supposed to have because it is going other places that it is not supposed to go.

Chapter 3

A Mountaintop Experience

Here am I and the children whom the *LORD has given me!* **We are for signs and wonders in Israel from the LORD of hosts, who dwells in Mount Zion.**

Isaiah 8:18

These are God's chosen people consecrated and set apart to praise and worship Him in consecrated worship. They could move closer to God's mountaintop where His lightning flashes and thunder rumbles. In the same way there are strategic guidelines that must be applied for us to approach Him if we want His power to reign in our lives. Moses is an excellent example of this. God told Moses that He was going to do something awesome through him. Then He gave him the keys to bring it to pass. We will look at the seven strategic keys in a later chapter.

And He said: "Behold, I make a covenant. Before all your people I will do marvels such as have not been done in all the earth, nor in any nation; and all the people among whom you are shall see the work of the LORD. For it is an awesome thing that I will do with you.

Exodus 34:10

The Burning Bush Experience

The Amplified Bible says, "I am going to do terrible things through you Moses. The people are going to marvel about what I am going to do through you." The world and its nations would never forget this Moses' mountaintop experience.

Now Moses was tending the flock of Jethro his father-in-law, the priest of Midian. And he led the flock to the back of the desert, and came to Horeb, the mountain of God.

And the Angel of the LORD appeared to him in a flame of fire from the midst of a bush. So he looked, and behold, the bush was burning with fire, but the bush was not consumed.

Then Moses said, "I will now turn aside and see this great sight, why the bush does not burn."

So when the LORD saw that he turned aside to look, God called to him from the midst of the bush and said, "Moses, Moses!" And he said, "Here I am."

Then He said, "Do not draw near this place. Take your sandals off your feet, for the place where you stand is holy ground."

Moreover He said, "I am the God of your father — the God of Abraham, the God of Isaac, and the God of Jacob." And Moses hid his face, for he was afraid to look upon God.

Exodus 3:1-6

Moses' encounter with God on this mountaintop was so life-changing that the Spirit of God within him always brought him back to this same mountain where he had his living Word experience (the Word like fire).

Moses was never the same after this point in his life. It was a divine place of contact, which became very strategic throughout his ministry.

As you read through the times in Moses' life you will see that many important things happened to him on this same mountaintop. This was the place where he received divine instruction from God to minister to the people. It was where he received the Ten Commandments and where he was transfigured, so his face shone with the glory of God. It was where God anointed Moses with power to work signs and wonders to let His people go.

Here am I and the children whom the LORD has given me! We are for signs and wonders in Israel from the LORD of hosts, who dwells in Mount Zion.
Isaiah 8:18

It is important that every individual come to a mountaintop experience!

Holy Ground

A mountaintop experience is a holy experience. God called Moses to do a powerful work from Mt. Horeb. Aaron challenged the power of this holy calling, which resulted in God's command to Moses to remove the mantle that was on Aaron's life, which took place on the mountain. The instant the mantle was removed Aaron died. Challenging the holy calling placed upon Moses, cost Aaron his life. (Numbers 20:28).

It was on another mountain that Elijah challenged the prophets of Baal. The prophets challenged the name of God and the holiness of God. As a result of this challenge, God was established in the high place of Mt. Carmel. The fire of God's purity answered the challenge and Elijah defeated the prophets on Mt. Carmel. Elijah was an anointed man of God who set up the altar of God in a high place upon Mt. Carmel (1 Kings 18). So it will be at the end of time.

We also face the devil today in the high places. Today, Baal's false prophets call themselves by such things as "psychics," and the day of encounters is at hand. I call it the battle of the gods.

"Then you call on the name of your gods, and I will call on the name of the LORD; and the God who answers by fire, He is God." So all the people answered and said, "It is well spoken."

1 King 18:24

Chapter 4
Battling for the High Places

"I can see, that there is coming from heaven new manifestations of the Holy Spirit in power and new manifestations will be in sweetness, in love, in tenderness beyond anything your heart or mine ever saw. The very lightning of God will flash through men's souls."
— *John G. Lake*

During Jesus' ministry, He shows us the place that John G. Lake is speaking of and more. Most of Jesus' life and ministry took place upon several mountains. *Jesus was tempted* on a mountain before entering into the fullness of His ministry. His most famous sermon is called the "Sermon on the Mount" because he taught it on the side of a mountain. Jesus was transfigured on the mountain. He healed the demoniac on the mountain. His last night on earth was spent on the Mount of Olives.

Our Lord's ministry was established and re-established in the high places. Mountains have often been called the holy place.[3]

Isaiah prophesies that every mountain and hill shall be made low (Isaiah 40:4). When Jesus comes back, Mount Olive will split (Zecharaiah 14:4). The term mountain can also be symbolic in the Bible of obstacles to God's power. God has removed all the obstacles, because through Jesus, redemption is complete. The question is, are we accepting and appropriating the completed work?

Battle of the Mind

The final battle in the body of Christ is being fought right now in the high places, on spiritual mountains beyond physical sight. Paul says our fight is with high things. And in any fight, someone loses. Paul laid out our battle plan to properly wage the fight.

For the weapons of our warfare are not carnal but mighty in God for pulling down strongholds,

casting down arguments and every high thing that exalts itself against the knowledge of God, bringing every thought into captivity to the obedience of Christ,

2 Corinthians 10:4,5

The high place fight is in the Christian's thought life. We are told to take dominion there. We are told to pull down Satan's thought strongholds before they affect or take root in our life.

If you don't deal with Satan's altars on the high places, you will accept immoral behavior, and it will become established as a high place in your life. We must destroy them, as Hezekiah and Josiah did.

"You shall not bow down to their gods, nor serve them, nor do according to their works; but you shall utterly overthrow them and completely break down their sacred pillars.

Exodus 23:24

'then you shall drive out all the inhabitants of the land from before you, destroy all their engraved stones, destroy all their molded images, and demolish all their high places...

Numbers 33:52

The High Places of Lust

King Solomon visited Satan's high place often, and he eventually fell prey to Satan's stronghold of immorality. First Kings 11:1-18 tells us His lust drove him to build altars upon the high places to worship other gods. He yielded to the desires of his wives. As a result, the kingdom was torn away from him.

But King Solomon loved many foreign women, as well as the daughter of Pharaoh: women of the Moabites, Ammonites, Edomites, Sidonians, and Hittites —

from the nations of whom the LORD had said to the children of Israel, "You shall not intermarry with them, nor they with you. Surely they will turn away your hearts after their gods." Solomon clung to these in love.

And he had seven hundred wives, princesses, and three hundred concubines; and his wives turned away his heart.

For it was so, when Solomon was old, that his wives turned his heart after other gods; and his heart was not loyal to the LORD his God, as was the heart of his father David.

For Solomon went after Ashtoreth the goddess of the Sidonians, and after Milcom the abomination of the Ammonites.

Solomon did evil in the sight of the LORD, and did not fully follow the LORD, as did his father David.

Then Solomon built a high place for Chemosh the abomination of Moab, on the hill that is east of Jerusalem, and for Molech the abomination of the people of Ammon.

And he did likewise for all his foreign wives, who burned incense and sacrificed to their gods.

1 Kings 11:1-8

Solomon's sin resulted in the division of the Hebrew nation.

So the LORD became angry with Solomon, because his heart had turned from the LORD God of Israel, who had appeared to him twice,

and had commanded him concerning this thing, that he should not go after other gods; but he did not keep what the LORD had commanded.

Therefore the LORD said to Solomon, "Because you have done this, and have not kept My covenant and My statutes, which I have commanded you, I will surely tear the kingdom away from you and give it to your servant.

"Nevertheless I will not do it in your days, for the sake of your father David; I will tear it out of the hand of your son.

"However I will not tear away the whole kingdom; I will give one tribe to your son for the sake of my servant David, and for the sake of Jerusalem which I have chosen."

1 Kings 11:9-13

Every Hebrew king was judged according to what they did in *the high places.*

Therefore they left the house of the LORD God of their fathers, and served wooden images and idols; and wrath came upon Judah and Jerusalem because of their trespass.

2 Chronicles 24:18

First and Second Kings tell the story of how so many of Solomon's successors fell to satan's high places. Every king in the Northern and many in the Southern Kingdom of Judah allowed the pagan worship of the nations surrounding them to seduce them away from God. Solomon intermarried with pagan wives and established the wicked high place practices for his many successors (1 Kings 3:3). God judged each king according to how they dealt with the high places. God will judge you the same way.

Remember, Asa initially removed some of the high places but didn't eliminate them.

Asa did what was right in the eyes of the LORD, as did his father David.

And he banished the perverted persons from the land, and removed all the idols that his fathers had made.

Also he removed Maachah his grandmother from being queen mother, because she had made an obscene image of Asherah. And Asa cut down her obscene image and burned it by the Brook Kidron.

But the high places were not removed. Nevertheless Asa's heart was loyal to the LORD all his days.
1 King 15:11-14

Look what happened because of not removing the high places.

Now there was war between Asa and Baasha king of Israel all their days.

And Baasha king of Israel came up against Judah, and built Ramah, that he might let none go out or come in to Asa king of Judah.

The rest of all the acts of Asa, all his might, all that he did, and the cities which he built, are they

not written in the book of the chronicles of the
kings of Judah? But in the time of his old age he
was diseased in his feet.

1 King 15:16,17,23

Whatever is Highest Receives the Power

When Israel set up their Asherah poles, the lightning of God would strike at the heart of their idolatry
because they were the highest objects. If there was any
of God's power released at all, it was released to judge
Israel's idolatry.

In the same way today, many only hear God's voice
in relation to the conviction of their sinful lives because
their idols have been raised highest in their lives.

Today we set up the poles of our high places in different ways. We put satellites into space and the pornography etc. beams down through television and over the
Internet to bring Asherah into our homes. Our fight
today is to turn off the switches of these conduits of evil
and allow them to be used as tools for Christ's wisdom
and goodness.

Whatever is highest in our lives will receive the
power. It will either flow through us or destroy us. I
don't care how big the preacher is, if there is ungodly
high place in his life, the fullness of power will not flow.

Whatever you as a modern day Christian do in the
high places will determine the weakness or the strength
of God in your life. If you are having problems with
imaginations and controlling your dreams at night, that
means there are still things in your high places that need
to be pulled down.

God will evaluate you according to what you do at
the high places. Why would God want to evaluate you
any differently than His biblical kings?

Once the battle for the high place is won, the place
of power will come.

Chapter 5
The Place of Power

Samuel went up from his city of Ramah to worship in Shiloh ("place of rest"), where the Ark of the Covenant and tabernacle were placed by Israel when possessing the Promised Land (see Joshua 1:18).

This man went up from his city yearly to worship and sacrifice to the LORD of hosts in Shiloh. Also the two sons of Eli, Hophni and Phinehas, the priests of the LORD, were there.

1 Samuel 1:3

Shiloh was a high place that was located in the city of Ramah on Mount Ephraim. Ramah means "hill", "a height", "high places of God" or to be "high." It was in this city that Samuel found Saul. This was a place of power. Great power takes place in the high places. It is also the place where the devil sets up his stronghold. Here he is speaking of reaching into the high places. Where did they go to worship? To Shiloh and Shiloh was a high place. There is a city called Ramah in Mount Ephraim. Shiloh was in this Mount Ephraim. Look what happens in the high places during this short period.

"As soon as you come into the city, you will surely find him before he goes up to the *high place* to eat. For the people will not eat until he

comes, because he must bless the sacrifice; afterward those who are invited will eat. Now therefore, go up, for about this time you will find him."

And Samuel answered Saul and said, "I am the seer. *Go up before me to the high place*, for you shall eat with me today; and tomorrow I will let you go and will tell you all that is in your heart.

1 Samuel 9:13,19

Why did Samuel want Saul to meet him in the high place? He was getting ready to pour oil upon Saul's head to confirm what God had already done. This had to be done in a strategic place. The anointing flows from the head down. The high place was strategic. It is strategic for the anointing to have free flow. Therefore, the high places must be dealt with. The consecration must be done in the high places in order for there to be a free flow of power. God had already anointed Saul before He was even born. God had already anointed Saul when choosing him. But the power had not come upon him yet. These verses are important in order to set up a strategic location for lightning to strike.

When they had come down from the high place into the city, Samuel spoke with Saul on the top of the house.

They arose early; and it was about the dawning of the day that Samuel called to Saul on the *top of the house*, saying, "Get up, that I may send you on your way." And Saul arose, and both of them went outside, he and Samuel.

As they were going down to the outskirts of the city, Samuel said to Saul, "Tell the servant to go on ahead of us." And he went on. "But you stand

here awhile, that I may announce to you the word of God."
1 Samuel 9:25-27

I want you to notice where this anointing is taking place. It is taking place on top of a house in Ramah, which means high places of God. You get anointed with God's power on His high places. There can't be any idolatry there when you get ready to ordain someone. The Bible says the Apostles prayed and fasted and then separated Barnabus and Paul. The reason they prayed and fasted was because they had to have everything in the high places clear of Satan's influence in order to anoint them for ministry.

The High Place is a Place of Ordination.

Now in the church that was at Antioch there were certain prophets and teachers: Barnabas, Simeon who was called Niger, Lucius of Cyrene, Manaen who had been brought up with Herod the tetrarch, and Saul.

As they ministered to the Lord and fasted, the Holy Spirit said, "Now separate to Me Barnabas and Saul for the work to which I have called them."

Then, having fasted and prayed, and laid hands on them, they sent them away.

So, being sent out by the Holy Spirit, they went down to Seleucia, and from there they sailed to Cyprus.
Acts 13:1-4

Then Samuel took a flask of oil and poured it on his head, and kissed him and said: "Is it not because the LORD has anointed you commander over His inheritance?
1 Samuel 10:1

But, the enemy is also at the high places. This is where he fights to rule. Read of the sons of the priest who raised Samuel (Hophni and Phineas), and you will discover Satan's religious power to pervert God's holy high place (1 Samuel 2:12, 22). The strategic stuff in your life for the power of God to flow is taking place in the high places.

"After that *you shall come to the hill of God* where the Philistine garrison is. And it will happen, when you have come there to the city, that you will meet a group of prophets coming down from the *high place* with a stringed instrument, a tambourine, a flute, and a harp before them; and they will be prophesying.

"Then the Spirit of the LORD will come upon you, and you will prophesy with them and be turned into another man.

"And let it be, when these signs come to you, that you do as the occasion demands; for God is with you."

1 Samuel 10:5-7

I want you to notice the first thing Saul did was he hooked himself up with the current move of God coming from the high places. He received impartation at the high places and now he is the conductor. He is now a strategic channel to administer God's power. Where did all this happen? It all happened in the high places. How was Saul turned into another man? He was now in a strategic position to administer God's power. He got hooked up with God in the high places. The supernatural began to manifest and God said now do as the occasion demands. Saul was supernaturally changed. What God wants to do through you and in you is going to happen in His high place. Saul received impartation on the mount and became a conductor of God's power. Once the power of God struck, he prophesied and became a strategic channel to administer God's power. The supernatural began to manifest and Samuel said, *"...do as the occasion demands; for God is with you."* Saul was supernaturally changed, and God wants to do the same with you.

When that power comes and is manifest in your life, you will know that you are in Divine contact, the Spirit of God will be upon you and you will prophesy, like Saul, and be turned into another man.

Chapter 6
Lightning

When the Lord directed me into a study on lightning, He revealed some fascinating connections between the natural occurrence of lightning, and His supernatural ways. I began thinking in terms of lightning rods and "stepped leaders" when thinking of anointing, power and kings. Read on, and I'll show you what I mean.

In 1749, Benjamin Franklin first suggested using "lightning rods" for the protection of buildings and barns.[4] Mr. Franklin proved how when a metal rod was placed at the apex of a structure and was grounded by a low resistance cable, it drew the power to it, protecting the structure it rested upon. In theory, the lightning strikes the rod and passes harmlessly into the ground. The rod's area of protection was a cone shaped space with a base radius equal to the height of the rod. But the rod's height had to be higher than the structure it was placed upon or the lightning would hit the structure the rod was placed to protect. The low resistance grounding cable, he discovered, was very important, because without a low resistance cable, whatever lightning strikes (lightning rods included) will be destroyed.

Franklin's rod proved that when lightning strikes, it looks for the highest point.

Lightning rods are common on modern buildings today. The height and extension of the rod is very strategic. It must be placed at the highest point. The higher the rod goes up, the greater sphere of protection it can cover.

Defining Lightning's Spiritual Connection

Our extension to the heavens must be at the highest point in the Lord. When it comes to the lightning of God striking through our being your ability to reach and abide in the heavenly realms and maintaining intimacy with God must be of greater value to you than anything else that you possess. The higher you go the wider the area will be that you will cover. This is also called apostolic authority. The higher a person rises apostolically in the dominion and call that God has called them to, their sphere of influence begins to maneuver and cover many people. It causes a strategic place for God's lightning to strike.

Lightning strikes can occur anytime the weather conditions permit it. The most familiar lightning strokes are the negative cloud to ground flashes.[5] They start near the base of a cloud in the form of an invisible discharge called the "stepped leader," which moves downward in discrete, microsecond steps about 165 ft long. The "stepped leader" is initiated by a small discharge near the cloud base, releasing the free electrons that move toward the ground. Then when rain begins to fall, electric discharges descend with the rain. It is at this point during a service that we begin to feel the presence and power of God. The cloud of glory covers the tabernacle and allows the glory of God to come in. God inhabits the praises of His people. We see in Second Chronicles 5 when Solomon began to worship God, how the cloud covered the tabernacle and the glory filled the temple. When they began to praise and worship God beneath the cloud, something began to be activated and discharged. The people begin to feel tingling in their hands, which is the tangible sensation of God's presence, which begins to open the door for the lightnings of God. The average interval between successive lightning strokes is 0.02 seconds and the average flash lasts 0.25 seconds. Because the duration of one powerful stroke is no more than 0.0002 seconds, the interval between strokes account for most of the duration of a lightning flash.

When the negatively charged "stepped leader" approaches to within 330 feet or 100 meters or less from the ground, a "leader" moves up from the ground away from protruding objects, such as buildings and trees to meet the "stepped leader" coming down. In my analogy, I discovered that God is the "stepped leader" and His worshippers are the "leaders" that connect from the ground. In order for lightning to hit the ground, it has to have a "step leader" going up. There has to be something activated from the ground releasing something that makes an extension to grab something that is coming down. This means that two things have to make contact. If the "stepped leader" and "ground leader" don't make contact in the natural, no lightning will occur. The protruding object is something that is in a high place. When the protruding object is hit with lightning, the object is destroyed. So what he does is he goes up this protruding object to get to the highest point.

Once the "step leaders" coming down and the "leaders" coming up have made contact, the visible lightning stroke, called the return stroke, flashes upward from the ground along the path of the "stepped leader." The "set leader" then sets up the path. It creates the channel once contact is made. He sets the guidelines for the path, how big the path will be and how much power will flow. Following the return stroke, several subsequent strokes can occur along the original main channel in less than seconds. These strokes continue until the charge center in the lower part of the cloud is eliminated. That is when praise and worship stopped going to God.

Once the "leaders" make contact, there is something on the ground that releases expectancy and a charge that tries to take hold of something coming down. The explosive heating and expansion of air along the "leader" path produces a shock wave that is heard as thunder. Thunder means that kings are making contact. We will look at thunder in the next chapter.

The analogy of this is stunning when you discover our praise is the "ground leader" and God's presence is the "stepped leader". When the protruding object of our praise stands up high, God's lightning strikes. God is waiting for a "leader" to rise and meet Him. When contact is made, lightning will strike and power will be revealed.

Studies with high-speed cameras have shown that most lightning flashes are multiple events, consisting of as many as forty-two main strokes, each of which is preceded by a "leader" stroke. All strokes follow an initial ionized path, which may be branched along with the current flows. The average interval between successive lightning strokes is 0.02 seconds and the average flash lasts 0.25 seconds. Because the duration of one powerful stroke is no more than 0.0002 seconds, the interval between strokes account for most of the duration of a lightning flash. The safest place during a lightning storm is inside a metal-bodied car or lying flat on the ground in the open. If you don't know Jesus then you had better get on your face when the power moves. This kind of power is going to hit the church and you had better not mess around with Peter or you will end up like Ananias and Sapphira. When this kind of power hits the church you will be on your face.

Lightning Replenishes the Earth

Lightning is good. Some scientists believe lightning is the key element that produced the simple elements and complex chemical compounds that make up life on earth. Every time it strikes, the soil is enriched with nitrogen that is released from the atmosphere and carried to the ground by raindrops.

Scientists also believe the reason why life under the ground is activated is because of lightning. When lightning hits the ground, electron charges release nitrogen into the ground. The released nitrogen then creates nitrates or salt. This is how salt gets in the earth.

The supernatural implications of this are very interesting. The Bible says His born-again church is the salt of the earth...and we can't be salt spiritually unless God's supernatural lightning strikes us. *Through us, the lightning of God can release His supernatural life throughout the earth.*

The Bible says the whole earth will be filled with the knowledge of His glory. Our "leader" from the bottom goes up the "stepped leader" from above and sets up as His power conductor. Are you ready?!!

The Manifestation

God makes a channel and He starts sending His lightning. When His lightning strikes through you, those people who are dead in this earth in sin and bondage are hit by His supernatural nitrogen and experience the goodness of God. God makes it very clear I will pour out My Spirit upon all flesh. The Bible makes it very clear that as lightning comes out of the east and shines even unto the west so shall the coming of the Son of Man be.

When Jesus returns, scripture says that He will look like lightning coming from the east and flashing to the west. In this prophetic verse His appearance, countenance, manifestation and actions all describe Jesus as lightning.

"For as the lightning comes from the east and flashes to the west, so also will the coming of the Son of Man be.   **Matthew 24:27**

The dispatched angel assigned to Jesus' resurrection is described as lightning in Matthew 28.

And behold, there was a great earthquake; for an angel of the Lord descended from heaven, and came and rolled back the stone from the door, and sat on it.

His countenance was like lightning, and his clothing as white as snow.

Matthew 28:2,3

And Daniel's revelation of Jesus describes Him as a burning lightning bolt.

His body was like beryl, his face like the appearance of lightning, his eyes like torches of fire, his arms and feet like burnished bronze in color, and the sound of his words like the voice of a multitude.

Daniel 10:6

The natural and supernatural connections of lightning to God are clear. When our praises reach His power, He releases Himself, Who is pictured over and over as lightning from on high.

Chapter 7

Seven Strategies for Moving in the Power of God

His brightness was like the light; he had rays flashing from His hand, and there His power was hidden.

Habakkuk 3:4

Once we establish our high place with God, we position ourselves to be rods of His power. We must choose to live holy and above the world's drawing. But we must draw near to Him, *presuming nothing* to show ourselves strong for Him. To ensure this in Israel's life, God gave Moses several strategies designed to be stepping stones that would lead the people to His high place. These strategies are still in place and will lead you to God's high place as you apply them.

"Observe what I command you this day. Behold, I am driving out from before you the Amorite and the Canaanite and the Hittite and the Perizzite and the Hivite and the Jebusite.

"Take heed to yourself, lest you make a covenant with the inhabitants of the land where you are going, lest it be a snare in your midst.

"But you shall destroy their altars, break their sacred pillars, and cut down their wooden images

"for you shall worship no other god, for the LORD, whose name is Jealous, is a jealous God),

"lest you make a covenant with the inhabitants of the land, and they play the harlot with their gods and make sacrifice to their gods, and one of them invites you and you eat of his sacrifice,

"and you take of his daughters for your sons, and his daughters play the harlot with their gods and make your sons play the harlot with their gods.

"You shall make no molded gods for yourselves.

                                    Exodus 34:11-17

In the above passage, God gave Moses seven directives that would ensure Israel's calling as His lightning rod.

1. **Obey My commandments (v. 11).**

2. **Do not compromise (v. 12).**

3. **Tear down all the altars (v. 13).**

4. **I want your absolute loyalty (v. 14).**

5. **I want your absolute exclusive devotion (v. 15).**

6. **Do not agree with spiritual prostitutes or hook up with those who are against Me (v. 16).**

7. **Don't receive impartation that I don't want you to receive (v. 17).**

God told Moses that He would do awesome things through him if the people would observe these seven things. The fornication and pagan teachings of the world became a snare to Israel historically because they rejected these seven strategies, just as much of the church does today. No, the church doesn't run down to the local sex cult like Israel eventually did. But one can commit spiritual fornication with philosophy, which will breed religious bondage and demons. This is where so much of the idolatry in our ranks finds itself today. So God began to immediately tear down the pagan altars that Egypt knew in order for mighty signs and wonders to take place. The same can happen through you today once you purge and make ready God's high place.

We Are God's Lightning Rods Stretched Between Heaven and Earth

God is dealing today with church compromise in the high places. He wants to release His lightning through His children. He wants to set mighty things into place. But before He can do that, we must submit to His authority and allow God to deal with the high places in our mind.

We need to be God's rod stretched between heaven and earth to connect the natural with the supernatural.

[He planned] for the maturity of the times and the climax of the ages to unify all things and head them up and consummate them in Christ [both] things in heaven and things on earth.

Ephesians 1:10 (AMP)

Our nature needs to be sensitive to the very power of God only then will all disease be destroyed. Like Moses, we can make contact and be used as God's conduit of miracles, signs and wonders in the earth.

And Moses said to Joshua, "Choose us some men and go out, fight with Amalek. Tomorrow I will stand on the top of the hill with the rod of God in my hand."

So Joshua did as Moses said to him, and fought with Amalek. And Moses, Aaron, and Hur went up to the top of the hill.

And so it was, when Moses held up his hand, that Israel prevailed; and when he let down his hand, Amalek prevailed.

But Moses' hands became heavy; so they took a stone and put it under him, and he sat on it. And Aaron and Hur supported his hands, one on one side, and the other on the other side; and his hands were steady until the going down of the sun.

Exodus 17:9-12

Notice in verse 12 that Aaron and Hur lifted up Moses' hands. His raised arms were symbolic of the contact Moses had established with heaven in God's high place. Because of this contact Israel prevailed over their enemies.

His lightning is ready to strike the church today. Our "leader" has risen from the ground. Jesus is saying, "My glory is going to fill the temple and something is about to strike. I am going to show Myself!" There are millions of people praising the Lord all over the world today, saying, "Lord, revive your works. His glory covered the heavens these are the clouds. All the electric charges are in place, positive and negative for the waves to go up and down and for the lightning to strike.

And when our praise leaders step up to His glory that covers the heavens, the electric charges of our praise will rise up and His lightning will strike. Notice the description of lightning by Habakkuk.

His flash is like the lightning; He has rays coming from His hand; And there it is that His strength is hidden.

Habakkuk 3:4 (ABPS)

In God's hand is lightning and hidden power. He awaits you in His high place. Humble yourself under the mighty hand of God, which can release His lightning and latter rain that will release His life in the earth. How awesome is the awesome omnipotent power of God!

Begin to Pray like Zechariah

Ask of the LORD rain in the time of the latter or spring rain. It is the LORD Who makes lightnings which usher in the rain and give men showers and grass to everyone in the field.

Zechariah 10:1 (AMP)

Have you ever seen anything stand in lightning's way? It digs a hole and clears everything out of its way. Nothing stops it. Psalm 97:4 says, "His lightning's light the world; the earth sees and trembles."

God is moving like lightning. He wants to strike and is looking for someone who won't resist His power. He wants to strike through you. He knows how and where to set up his channel, as he explained to Job.

"Who has divided a channel for the overflowing water, or a path for the thunderbolt,

to cause it to rain on a land where there is no one, a wilderness in which there is no man..."

Job 38:25,26

"My lightning causes rain in the land and in the wilderness, and I make it happen. Do you understand this Job?" And today God is asking you if you really understand this kind of power. You are the Lord's channel to send up a "ground leader" and connect with His "stepped leader" to conduct God's lightning power to the earth. Now rise and begin to worship and praise Him. Begin to make divine contact.

Do you know the ordinances of the heavens? Can you set their dominion over the earth?

"Can you lift up your voice to the clouds, that an abundance of water may cover you?

Job 38:33,34

When you commit to His high place and worship Him, the power in His hands will be released. Lighting will strike. In these verses God is talking about the keys to the kingdom, which correlates with the ordinances of heaven. Understanding the heavenlies is one of the keys to the kingdom. When you get a revelation of lightning, you have received a key to the kingdom. The "stepped leader" is setting up a clear pathway. God is asking Job: "Can you worship Me until there is a discharge, until a "leader" rises from the earth to meet the "leader" coming down and unlock my power from on high to ignite and water the earth? When you praise and worship Him, the power in His hands will be released and lightning will strike.

Can you send out lightnings, that they may go, and say to you, 'Here we are!'?

Job 38:35

Here We Are!

Here we are! I have just showed up. The Old Testament is a shadow. When Jesus was transfigured divine contact was made. When Jesus went up on the mountain to the high places His clothes became white as lightning and the glory of God shown all about Him. This is the essence of power, which is the unity in lightning. It is the Father, the Son and the Holy Spirit all making contact. *Here we are.* Can you send out lightning and say here we are? Jesus went on top of the mountain and became the lightning rod making contact with heaven. He had contact. When you see the lightning, you can see me. Here we are, I am showing Myself powerful. It is the essence of who God really is.

Lightning represents the essence of the Father, the Son and the Holy Spirit. They are three in one manifesting together at the same time. When all three of them hit each other in unity you see a manifestation of lightning. Lightning reveals something that overrides everything else in the universe. Jesus is giving us a revelation of His unity. God is saying, Job, I am trying to show you something. Can you lift up your voice into the clouds where the abundance of water is? He is saying come up to Me, can you do it? Can you send out lightning and say, here we are? God is saying I send out lightning and we say here we are, we just showed up. Can you do that? God is saying in Christ dwells the fullness of the godhead bodily. *Here we are.* God with us! **God is about to release the kind of revelation that says, "Here I am."** There isn't anybody else. You are going to know that I am here. When Jesus shows up you know He is there.

Now after six days Jesus took Peter, James, and John his brother, led them up on a high mountain by themselves;

and He was transfigured before them. His face shone like the sun, and His clothes became as white as the light.

And behold, Moses and Elijah appeared to them, talking with Him.

Then Peter answered and said to Jesus, "Lord, it is good for us to be here; if You wish, let us make here three tabernacles: one for You, one for Moses, and one for Elijah."

While he was still speaking, behold, a bright cloud overshadowed them; and suddenly a voice

came out of the cloud, saying, *"This is My beloved Son, in whom I am well pleased. Hear Him!"*

Matthew 17:1-5

When Jesus was transfigured, we see the unity of the Father, the Son and the Holy Spirit and we hear the wonderful voice of the Father.

Chapter 8
Thunder

You called in trouble, and I delivered you; I answered you in the secret place of thunder; I tested you at the waters of Meribah. Selah

Psalm 81:7

These scriptures show us that God's secret place is in the middle of thunder. I have experienced the reality of this many times, as I lay in my bed at night in hotel rooms praying. I have called on God, consciously giving Jesus Christ all the power of my spirit, mind and body — and His lightning has struck. It felt like thunder and lightning came into the room, like the sonic boom of concord jet! Massively loud and humbling, I've felt bolts of power shoot through my body for about forty-five minutes, helpless to do anything until it was over. The services that have followed these high place encounters have been full of massive power. He has answered me in the secret place of thunder. It is not a quiet place.

The connection between thunder and lightning is a powerful disclosure of God's manifestation in other revelations of Scripture as well. Thunder is the sound that follows a flash of lightning.[6] Its sound and feeling speaks of the presence of God.

"Have you an arm like God? Or can you thunder with a voice like His?"

43

There is probably no better known power connection of God in the gospels related to this study, than the recorded occurrence of thunder. When Jesus predicted His death on the cross, a voice came from heaven as a seal of approval upon His redemptive mission. Some people who heard the heavenly voice said that it had thundered; others said, "An angel has spoken to Him"

"Now My soul is troubled, and what shall I say? 'Father, save Me from this hour'? But for this purpose I came to this hour.

"Father, glorify Your name." Then a voice came from heaven, saying, "I have both glorified it and will glorify it again."

Therefore the people who stood by and heard it said that it had thundered. Others said, "An angel has spoken to Him."
John 12:27-29

When Moses stretched his rod toward heaven, the Lord sent thunder and hail as the seventh plague upon the land of Egypt.

And Moses stretched out his rod toward heaven; and the LORD sent thunder and hail, and fire darted to the ground. And the LORD rained hail on the land of Egypt.
Exodus 9:23

The Lord sent thunder at the giving of the law at Mount Sinai.

Then it came to pass on the third day, in the morning, that there were thunderings and lightnings and a thick cloud on the mountain; and the sound of the trumpet was very loud, so that all the people who were in the camp trembled.

Exodus 19:16

Now all the people witnessed the thunderings, the lightning flashes, the sound of the trumpet and the mountain smoking; and when the people saw it, the trembled and stood afar off.

Exodus 20:18

Thunder exploded when the Philistines drew near to battle against Israel.

Now as Samuel was offering up the burnt offering, the Philistines drew near to battle against Israel. But the LORD thundered with a loud thunder upon the Philistines that day, and so confused them that they were overcome before Israel.

1 Samuel 7:10

Thunder seldom occurred during Palestine's long, dry summer (mid-April through mid-September). This scarcity meant that it naturally became a symbol of God's power, wrath and vengeance. When Samuel called upon the Lord, thunder and rain came during the wheat harvest (a notoriously dry season), and the people greatly feared the Lord.

"Is today not the wheat harvest? I will call to the LORD, and He will send thunder and rain, that you may perceive and see that your wickedness is great, which you have done in the sight of the LORD, in asking a king for yourselves."

So Samuel called to the LORD, and the LORD sent thunder and rain that day; and all the people greatly feared the LORD and Samuel.

1 Samuel 12:17,18

David witnessed God's thunder in his prophecy of deliverance.

"The LORD thundered from heaven, and the Most High uttered His voice.

He sent out arrows and scattered them; lightning bolts, and He vanquished them.

Samuel 22:14,15

And the Book of Revelation is *full* of prophetic references to God's presence in both lightning and thunder.

And from the throne proceeded lightnings, thunderings, and voices. Seven lamps of fire were burning before the throne, which are the seven Spirits of God.

Revelation 4:5

And I heard a voice from heaven, like the voice of many waters, and like the voice of loud thunder. And I heard the sound of harpists playing their harps.

Revelation 14:2

And I heard, as it were, the voice of a great multitude, as the sound of many waters and as the sound of mighty thunderings, saying, "Alleluia! For the Lord God Omnipotent reigns!

Revelation 19:6

The return of Jesus Christ is also revealed through the power of a lightning strike from heaven.

"For as the lightning that flashes out of one part under heaven shines to the other part under heaven, so also the Son of Man will be in His day.

Luke 17:24

Ezekiel reveals living creatures that streak across the heavens like lightning.

As for the likeness of the living creatures, their appearance was like burning coals of fire, and like the appearance of torches. Fire was going back and forth among the living creatures; the fire was bright, and out of the fire went lightning.

Ezekiel 1:13

Then the LORD will be seen over them, and His arrow will go forth like lightning. The Lord GOD will blow the trumpet, and go with whirl-winds from the south.

Zechariah 9:14

The voice of Your thunder was in the whirl-wind; the lightnings lit up the world; the earth trembled and shook.

Psalms 77:18

This shaking that is common to thunder is very strategic.

"Now, Lord, look on their threats, and grant to Your servants that with all boldness they may speak Your word,

"by stretching out Your hand to heal, and that signs and wonders may be done through the name of Your holy Servant Jesus."

And when they had prayed, the place where they were assembled together was shaken; and they were all filled with the Holy Spirit, and they spoke the word of God with boldness.

Acts 4:29-31

God wants to touch and minister through your hands. There is a resident power. God has come to make His dwelling place in you. God answers you in the secret place of thunder. That doesn't sound like the secret place is a quiet place. When lightning strikes it makes a lot of noise. You will hear God very clear.

Get ready, God is releasing lightning power and the sound of thunder will echo around the world.

Chapter 9
Making Contact

Who is he who condemns? It is Christ who died, and furthermore is also risen, who is even at the right hand of God, who also makes intercession for us.

Romans 8:34

Jesus is at the right hand of the Father in His high place of worship making intercession for you at this very moment, and His intercession will come to pass. The Holy Spirit is down here within His people making intercession. Between Jesus making intercession and the Holy Spirit making intercession, a channel for His power is dynamically set up. The Spirit of God within you is the "leader" Who desires to rise up to meet the "step leader" of God in the heavens. The Spirit inside you makes Divine contact. Prayer is God working with God.[7]

For there is one God and one Mediator between God and men, the Man Christ Jesus,

1 Timothy 2:5

The Holy Spirit within us prays when we're too weak to make Divine contact with the Father's "leader" from above so there can be harmony in the Spirit. When your resistance to Him is low, He can easily work through you you as His rod to call those things, which are not as though they are concerning your life. He makes intercession for us with groanings that cannot be uttered. "I have to go up!," Is the Spirit's constant cry. "I have to be one with Jesus!"

Likewise the Spirit also helps in our weaknesses. For we do not know what we should pray for as we ought, but the Spirit Himself makes intercession for us with groanings which cannot be uttered.

Now He who searches the hearts knows what the mind of the Spirit is, because He makes intercession for the saints according to the will of God.

Romans 8:26, 27

For with stammering lips and another tongue he will speak to this people...

Isaiah 28:11

Jesus is Still Praying for You

You are the temple of God, the Spirit of God dwells inside of you. That is why David prayed, revive us and activate us. Do something alive in me. "Quicken me according to Your Word, give life to me." You need to learn to receive the intercession of Jesus. He is interceding for you but some people are not receiving what He is interceding for. Thank you Jesus that you are standing in the gap setting a channel into place for me. I receive that intercession. Let that lightning strike through me. Let that nitrogen, that energy from heaven, the power of God brings life into your people. I have to receive that. When I receive that there is discharge. God is trying to set up a divine channel through you. You have been set apart by God. You are a child of the Most High. You are a King. You are a royal priesthood. You have been given authority and power. It abides in you.

But you are a chosen generation, a royal priesthood, a holy nation, His own special people, that you may proclaim the praises of Him who called you out of darkness into His marvelous light;

1 Peter 2:9

Do you not know that you are the temple of God and that the Spirit of God dwells in you?

1 Corinthians 3:16

You Are God's Temple

Today God's temple is not located in some high place in the Hills of Ramah or on the temple mount in Jerusalem. You are the temple of God, the Spirit of God dwells inside of you.

Or do you not know that your body is the temple of the Holy Spirit who is in you, whom you have from God, and you are not your own?

For you were bought at a price; therefore glorify God in your body and in your spirit, which are God's.

1 Corinthians 6:19,20

The awesomeness of God's power is amazing. He is calling us up. Come to Me. Come run on the mountains with Me.

Then we will not turn back from You; revive us, and we will call upon Your name.

Psalms 80:18

Revive us. Activate the Holy Spirit. When I know not what to pray for the Spirit makes groaning, which cannot be uttered. He is trying to take you somewhere.

God is the power source resident in you, available at your command. That lines up exactly with First Samuel 10:7 when Saul came up to the mountains where the prophets were and he told Saul to go, do whatever the occasion demands. How can you do whatever the occasion demands if God doesn't give you resident power? I have given you the anointing from the Holy One who knows all things. I have given you unction from the Holy One who abides in you and teaches you all things. I have given you residential abiding power. I am waiting for you to release the commands. I am waiting for you to stretch forth your hand. I am waiting for you to open your mouth.

But you, beloved, building yourselves up on your most holy faith, praying in the Holy Spirit,

Jude 1:20

Therefore He is also able to save to the uttermost those who come to God through Him, since He always lives to make intercession for them.

Hebrews 7:25

So pray in the Spirit daily, and learn to receive the intercession of Jesus. Your spiritual praise can reach up to heaven today. This is always transpiring in God's high, heavenly place. He is interceding for you. Thank Him daily that He is standing in the gap, setting a channel into place for you.

For Christ has not entered the holy places made with hands, which are copies of the true, but into heaven itself, now to appear in the presence of God for us;

Hebrews 9:24

When His temples in Paul and Silas were thrown into a physical prison, they chose to meet God on His high place, and His high place thundered down.

But at midnight Paul and Silas were praying and singing hymns to God, and the prisoners were listening to them.

Suddenly there was a great earthquake, so that the foundations of the prison were shaken; and immediately all the doors were opened and everyone's chains were loosed.

Acts 16:25,26

When Lightning Strikes, Things Get Shaken

"Leaders" on the earth were making divine contact. When lightning strikes there is a shaking. Do you know what happened? They got absolutely set free. But they were doing something. They were praising and worshiping God. When you release praise and love to God you release God to Himself. *His "leader"* comes down from heaven waiting for a "leader" to rise from the earth, and He recognizes Himself. He knows when there has been Divine contact, and He sets up a path for His lightning to strike. We need to be the rod stretched between heaven and Earth. Paul and Silas were His rods stretched up to meet Him in the air. You be a rod of His contact, and He will shake the world through you.

Allow the lightning of God to strike through you. Let His nitrogen energy from heaven bring life to those you are in contact with here below. When it happened through God's lightning rods in that Philippian prison, everyone was set free. Paul and Silas allowed their "leaders" of praise to ascend to connect with God, and

Boom! The foundations of the prison were shaken, and the prisoners were set free.

It is time for the church to understand how to connect the natural with the supernatural. It is time to become sensitive to God's power. There is day coming from heaven on which the manifestation of God's power will be so sweet and full of love that it will electrify those who will receive it. His lightning will be so irrefutable and full of His tenderness, that He will flash His love through men's souls.

Intimacy in High Places

But you must prepare His high place so your ability to have intimacy with Him is greater than any other ability that you have. *That means your ability to extend and enter the presence of God must be far greater than any vision or desire you have.* If you want God to strike through your being, you will have to give Him freely all the powers of your spirit, mind and body. Remember, His lightning hits the highest objects and if you aren't high enough then lightning won't hit you. Some people's connection, intimacy and relationship with God is not high enough. They say God I want your power to flow through me, but personal intimacy with God is weak.

In order for the lightning of God to strike through your being, your ability to reach and abide, maintaining intimacy with Jesus Christ must be the greatest thing that you have ever done in your life. Make a new commitment today to reach up to and abide in His heavenly realm, maintaining intimacy with Jesus Christ as the central focus of your life. Set up your tower as high as you can go.

Enoch's relationship with God in His high place was so intimate that he walked and talked with God, and he "was not." Why? His priority was to maintain intimacy and a divine contact with God. That sets up the channel for the power of God.

> **And Enoch** *walked with God*; **and he was not, for God took him.**
> **Genesis 5:24**

Remember Enoch's first ministry was to walk with God.

Low Resistance

When a lightning rod is set up, it must have a low resistant cable that allows the full charge of lightning to be absorbed or the pole it hits will be completely fried. That is why they set in place a low resistant cable, because that power has to go into the ground. You cannot handle that kind of power and have any kind of resistance in your life. That is one of the reasons that kind of power doesn't flow in the body yet in full measure. There are hindrances to the power moving. We need to be the rod stretched between heaven and earth. The same is true on a spiritual plane. You can't handle the kind of power God wants to unleash if you have any kind of resistance in your life. Enoch had none. This is the reason His life ended in supernatural splendor.

We are the doorways to God's power, so our raised poles must be grounded, like Enoch's, with low resistance to His purposes and plans. It is when we refuse God's "stepped leader" of full devotion and worship, that high resistance refuses His will. It is up to us to submit and live out God's holy, shaking will.

> **See that you do not refuse Him who speaks. For if they did not escape who refused Him who spoke on earth, much more shall we not escape if we turn away from Him who speaks from heaven,**

whose voice then shook the earth; but now He has promised, saying, "Yet once more I shake not only the earth, but also heaven."

Now this, "Yet once more," indicates the removal of those things that are being shaken, as of things that are made, that the things which cannot be shaken may remain.

Therefore, since we are receiving a kingdom which cannot be shaken, let us have grace, by which we may serve God acceptably with reverence and godly fear.

For our God is a consuming fire.

Hebrews 12:25-29

The shaking that opened the Philippian prison through Paul and Silas' lightning rods of worship revealed God's sovereign power and led the jailer to God. Paul knew God's high place of power. And God is waiting for others like him to rise and make contact as conduits of His power. Divine contact must be made to enter His realm of the supernatural.

Intimacy is the Key

The enemy can't touch you when you dwell in the intimacy of God's high place. Can you imagine Satan climbing Mt. Horeb to frustrate the power and plans of God? It couldn't happen. He had to attack the people who were at the foot of the mountain, outside of God's presence. And this is how it remains today.

Let us become a mighty army of mountaintop warriors today who put the enemy to flight in fear and trembling. Israel's promise of Satan's scattering, is our promise today:

"The LORD will cause your enemies who rise against you to be defeated before your face; they shall come out against you one way and flee before you seven ways. Deuteronomy 28:7

The true Christian lives with demons screaming and running in terror of coming within a hundred yards from them. You have been given authority and power to tread upon serpents and scorpions and over all the power of the enemy

"Behold, I give you the authority to trample on serpents and scorpions, and over all the power of the enemy, and nothing shall by any means hurt you." Luke 10:19

God wants to do something powerful through you. Stop arguing over where God wants you to go. He wants to meet with you on His high place. GO! Lower your resistance to his empowering charge. Allow yourself, as Moses did, to be His conduit for the greater signs and wonders to move.

Then the LORD said to Moses, "Stretch out your hand over the sea, that the waters may come back upon the Egyptians, on their chariots, and on their horsemen."

And Moses stretched out his hand over the sea; and when the morning appeared, the sea returned to its full depth, while the Egyptians were fleeing into it. So the LORD overthrew the Egyptians in the midst of the sea. Exodus 14:26,27

God has called you, just like Moses. Accept His call today.

Chapter 10
Conclusion

A nd He said: "Behold, I make a covenant. Before all your people I will do marvels such as have not been done in all the earth, nor in any nation; and all the people among whom you are shall see the work of the LORD. For it is an awesome thing that I will do with you.

Exodus 34:10

One last word of encouragement I must give you in this final chapter has to do with your root inner desires that are demonstrated by your words, actions and goals. God's Word will do exactly what it says. But you must commit to practice it, focus in and extend yourself to heaven, and choose to worship Him. When you do, He will break any hindering barriers that are blocking His flow in your life to use you as His rod in bringing others to the light.

The problem is, we always want someone to wave a magic wand while we sin. But it doesn't work that way. You have to change something. God is looking to work with Himself in you. This is where our low resistance cable analogy applies strategically. As you apply the seven strategies listed in chapter 5, you will install a spiritual low resistance cable that invites Him to release His lightning through you. If He is going to strike, He needs an avenue to flow. Set a goal in your life to be used of God. Let the seven strategies for obedience guide you toward achievement, and your actions and words will be pleasing in His sight.

Allow the truth of Colossians 2:8-10 to direct you in seeking and staying in God's high place, day and night.

See to it that no one carries you off as spoil or makes you captive by so called philosophy and intellectualism and vain deceit, plain nonsense, fancies following human traditions, mans ideas and thoughts of material rather than the spiritual world. Just crude notions following the rudimentary elementary regarding the teachings of Christ the Messiah.

For in Him the whole fullness of Diety (the Godhead) continues to dwell in bodily form [giving complete expression of the divine nature]

And you are in Him, made full and having come to fullness of life [in Christ you too are filled with the Godhead — Father, Son and Holy Spirit- and reach full spiritual stature]. And He is the head of all rule and authority [of every angelic principality and power].

Colossians 2:8-10 (AMP)

Serve God, Not Satan, in Your High Place

Stay out of Satan's lying deceptions of religion, and draw near to Christ, Who is the fullness of life in which you have been made full. Let your praises ascend into heaven from His Spirit who lives in you to connect with God's "leader", Who releases His lightning to flow. Do it every day. Make this your goal. Whatever pattern you set up in your mind will bring forth the knowledge of the glory of God to let His Sword of the Spirit manifest in your life. Give God all the resources of your flesh, soul, and mind by first climbing up the mountain to pull down any strongholds that have been hindering you.

Then, once you make serving in God's high place the focus of your life, make sure your words and actions line up with that vision, or Satan will very subtly reclaim the high ground in your life. Don't compromise. Speak the Word of God: not Satan's.

Don't Compromise Your Commitment

You will be tempted to compromise your commitment. So speak the Word of God when Satan comes. If you can't pass the temptation of the flesh and the soul then you will never pass the temptation of the spirit — now rise up and be bold.

The enemy will flee when you speak in faith. If you speak in mere hope, he will dialogue with you to be more reasonable about compromising the holiness of your high place, and before you know it, the old worldly, religious mindset will try to creep in.

Make it your goal to do whatever it takes to abide in God's high place so He can flow through you. Watch over that goal by committing to remove anything that is hindering His flow through you. When you recognize any resistance, take authority over it and bind it. Speak God's Word. Strip it away. Sometimes the Spirit will lead you to pray and fast. Do it. Allow yourself to be His conduit in a powerful, fiery way. Moses prayed and fasted. So did Jesus. So did Paul and Silas. And so must you.

And always remember that you are called to touch other people. When the lightning of God strikes you, He will move you to set other men free.

And the keeper of the prison, awaking from sleep and seeing the prison doors open, supposing the prisoners had fled, drew his sword and was about to kill himself.

But Paul called with a loud voice, saying, "Do yourself no harm, for we are all here."

Then he called for a light, ran in, and fell down trembling before Paul and Silas.

And he brought them out and said, "Sirs, what must I do to be saved?"

So they said, "Believe on the Lord Jesus Christ, and you will be saved, you and your household."

Then they spoke the word of the Lord to him and to all who were in his house.

Acts 16:27-32

Final Thought

The experience of releasing the tangible anointing into others to see burdens removed and yokes destroyed is a humbling experience. But even more I desire to know the consistency of the lightning power of God striking through individuals delivering them, seeing the fullness of God's creative power rule.

Now pray this prayer!

Father, I come before you as your son/daughter and I believe you have called me to walk in your fullness. I thank You for the blood of Christ that purges my conscience from all dead works and all forms of resistance to the fullness of your power. I thank you that I am seated in heavenly places with You and enjoy the fullness of intimacy with you.

Now, Lord, look on their threats, and grant to Your servants that with all boldness they may speak your word,

by stretching out Your hand to heal, and that signs and wonders may be done through the name of Your holy Servant Jesus.

And when they had prayed, the place where they were assembled together was shaken; and they were all filled with the Holy Spirit, and they spoke the word of God with boldness.

Acts 4: 29-31

Habakkuk 2:2,3 "Then the LORD answered me and said: 'Write the vision and make it plain on tablets,that he may run who reads it. For the vision is yet for an appointed time, but at the end it will speak, and it will not lie. Though it tarries, wait for it; because it will surely come, it will not tarry.'"

The Prophet Habakkuk was waiting expectantly for the vision and as he waited, God answered. Look at verse 14, "For the earth will be filled with the knowledge of the glory of the LORD, as the waters cover the sea."

I believe the results of his first prayer activated his spirit to pray even stronger. Then in Habakkuk 3, the prophet Habakkuk prays, "A prayer of Habakkuk the prophet, on Shigoinoth O LORD, I have heard your speech and was afraid; O LORD, revive Your work in the midst of the years! In the midst of the years make it known, in wrath remember mercy." His brightness was like the light, he had rays flashing from His hand, and there His power was hidden.

Now all the people witnessed the thunderings, the lightning flashes, the sound of the trumpet, and the mountain smoking; and when the people saw it, they trembled and stood afar off.

Then they said to Moses, "You speak with us, and we will hear; but let not God speak with us, lest we die."

And Moses said the the people, 'Do not fear; for God has come to test you, and that His fear may be before you, so that you may not sin."

So the people stood afar off, but Moses drew near the thick darkness where God was.

Exodus 20:18-21

Don't be like the children of Israel, afraid to come face to face with God. Experience His thundering and lightning for yourself.

Father, I humble myself under Your mighty hand and I yield to the release of your lightning power.

"Ask of the LORD rain in the time of the latter or spring rain. It is the LORD Who makes lightnings which usher in the rain and give men showers and grass to everyone in the field."

Zechariah 10:1 (AMP)

---

[1] *Bibliography Albright William Foxwell, Yahweh and the Gods of Canaan. A Historical Analysis of Two Contrasting Faiths.* Garden City, NY Doubleday, & Co, INC. 1968 page 1719

[2] (from *International Standard Bible Encyclopedia,* Electronic Database Copyright © 1996 by Biblesoft).

[3] For more information on this please see Warren Hunter's book called *A Place Called Mt Olivet.*

[4] *Microsoft Encarta Encyclopedia 97,* 1993-1996 Microsoft Corporation

[5] *Microsoft Encarta Encyclopedia 97,* 1993-1996 Microsoft Corporation

[6] *Nelson's Illustrated Bible Dictionary* Copyright © 1986, Thomas Nelson

[7] For more information read my book, *God Working With God Through Prayer.*

We Would Like To Hear From You!

My staff and I at Sword Ministries believe that through reading this book you were touched by the power and glory of God. It is important to us and to the Lord that you let us know what wonderful things God is doing for you, and how your life was changed. Please send us your testimony so others can see what God has done for you. We would love to hear from you soon and we look forward to reading your testimony.

In addition, we would also like you to pray about becoming a *VISIONARY COVENANT PARTNER* with all of us at Sword Ministries International. As you join with us, it will enable us to touch more lives with the power and glory of God. In Philippians chapter 4, Paul speaks about becoming a partaker of grace. As you become a part of this ministry in prayer and finances you will become a partaker of the grace that God has given to us.

As you pray, we believe that you will be sensitive to the leading of the Holy Spirit on whether you are to become a part of this ministry. We believe that you have been blessed mightily by this book and believe that your life has been changed. To become a vital part of this ministry please fill out this form and send it with your prayer request and financial support to the address on the following page.

Keys That Will Unlock the Kingdom

Keys to a Yielded Will

In a fresh new light, Warren Hunter explores biblical truth's that will help individuals become vessels that are completely yielded and ready for the greatest outpouring of His spirit the world has ever seen.

$7.00

Presenting a Yielded Will

In the sequel to "Keys to a Yielded Will", Warren reveals how our salvation really hung in the balance of Jesus' life. One single act of disobedience would have nullified the power of His sacrifice. How many people are hanging in the balance at this time? Waiting on the obedience of our yielded will?

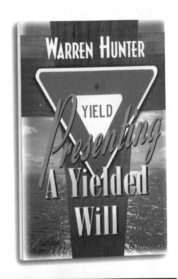

$8.00

ORDER FORM

Name_____

Address_____

City_____

State_____ Zip _____

Credit Card# _____

Exp Date_____Visa_____MC_____

Visionary Covenant Partner

☐ I would like to become a Visionary Covenant Partner.
Enclosed is my first gift of...

☐ 25   ☐ 50   ☐ 100   ☐ 250
☐ 500   ☐ 750   ☐ 1000   ☐ 5000

Or Other $_____ (Please fill in amout in Partner Gift Below)

		Shipping & Handling USA Only
Product Cost	$ _____	Under $10...........Add $2.00
S&H	$ _____	$10-$20..................Add $4.00
Sub Total	$ _____	$21-$30..................Add $6.00
Partner Gift	$ _____	$31-$40..................Add $7.00
		$41-$50..................Add $8.00
Total Enclosed	$ _____	$51 and Up..........Add 15%

Return Policy: Return any Defective Merchandise within 15 days of receipt.
PLEASE ALLOW 4 - 6 WEEKS FOR DELIVERY
ALL ORDERS MUST BE PREPAID

Clip & Mail To:

SWORD MINISTRIES
PMB 649
3044 Shepherd of the Hills Exprwy # 100
Branson, MO 65616
Phone: 417-335-7650 • Fax: 417-334-2003
E-mail Address: SWORD352@AOL.COM
World Wide Web: www.swordministries.org

Single Tapes

	Full of New Wine	$5.00
	The Ultimate Weapon	$5.00
	Journey of the Glory	$5.00
	The Breath of God	$5.00
	Divine Compassion	$5.00
	5 A's & 3 R's	$5.00
	In Christ Dwells Fulness	$5.00
	Take Time to Get Fire	$5.00
	The Promised Seal	$5.00
	New Testament Church	$5.00
	Unlimited Seed of Christ	$5.00
	Controlling Your Dreams	$5.00
	Proclaiming Christ	$5.00
	Voice of the Lord	$5.00
	Fueling for Fire	$5.00
	Praying for Revival	$5.00
	Flames of Intercession	$5.00
	Ephesians 1:18	$5.00
	Face to Face	$5.00
	Heart to Heart	$5.00
	The Hand of God	$5.00
	Preach Christ	$5.00
	Anointed Blood	$5.00
	Anointed Body	$5.00
	Sanctified Tongue	$5.00
	Sanctified Body	$5.00
	Glory of Hope	$5.00
	Called Out of The Familiar	$5.00

Single Tapes cont.

	Seeing Impartation	$5.00
	Seeing Past Death	$5.00
	Foundation for Prayer	$5.00
	Spread Your Wings	$5.00
	Cornelius Doorway to Power	$5.00
	Walk on the Water	$5.00
	Wrapped in His Presence	$5.00
	The Eagle Speaks	$5.00
	Redemptive Revelation -K. Hunter	$5.00
	What are You Yoked With -K.Hunter	$5.00
	Valleys -K.Hunter	$5.00
	Identifying the Gehazi -K.Hunter	$5.00
	Faith Without Works is Dead -K.Hunter	$5.00
	The Battle of the Gods	$5.00
	The Ultimate Decision	$5.00
	First Fruits	$5.00
	A Giving Eye	$5.00
	Seed of Covenant	$5.00
	Personhood of the Glory	$5.00

Books

	Keys To A Yielded Will	$7.00
	Presenting A Yielded Will	$8.00
	Unlimited Realm Vol. 1	$7.00
	From Fire To Glory	$10.00
	Transparency	$7.00
	Is Your Perception A Weapon?	$8.00
	Growing In Confidence	$7.00
	Power Of A Consecrated Heart	$7.00

Books cont.

	Supply Of The Spirit	$8.00
	Touch Not Mine Anointed	$6.00
	Vision Of The Seed	$6.00
	Glory Of The Anointing	$7.00
	Weightiness of God	$6.00
	Visionaries Rise To Leadership	$7.00
	Visionaries Set Your Sights Higher	$7.00
	Unlimited Realm Vol. 2	$7.00
	Buy All 16 Books and Save 30% Off!	$80.00

Album Tape Sets   Buy Any 3 and Get 20% Off!

	16 Classic Tapes	16 Tapes	$70.00
	Moving in Supernatural	16 Tapes	$70.00
	Power of Covenant	15 Tapes	$65.00
	Secrets of Financial Freedom	12 Tapes	$60.00
	God Working With God	12 Tapes	$60.00
	Be Son of God You Are	10 Tapes	$50.00
	Called to Call	10 Tapes	$50.00
	Meditating God's Thoughts	9 Tapes	$45.00
	Love's Perception	9 Tapes	$45.00
	Mirror of Grace	8 Tapes	$40.00
	Following the Cloud	8 Tapes	$40.00
	Anointed Ones Anointing	8 Tapes	$40.00
	Love's Destiny	8 Tapes	$40.00
	Financial Dominion	8 Tapes	$40.00
	Transparency	7 Tapes	$35.00
	Visionary Leadership	7 Tapes	$35.00
	Manifesting Life	7 Tapes	$35.00
	Yield To Healing	7 Tapes	$35.00
	Supply of The Spirit	7 Tapes	$35.00

Album Tape Sets   Buy Any 3 and Get 20% Off!

	Growing In Revival	6 Tapes	$30.00
	Recovery of Sight to the Blind	6 Tapes	$30.00
	Fruity Weapons **NEW!**	6 Tapes	$30.00
	Come Forth to Power	6 Tapes	$30.00
	Healing Absolutes	6 Tapes	$30.00
	New Realms of Vision	6 Tapes	$30.00
	Don't Abort A Miracle	6 Tapes	$30.00
	Fire to Glory	6 Tapes	$30.00
	Emanating the Anointing	6 Tapes	$30.00
	Apostolic Power Base	6 Tapes	$30.00
	Apostolic Patterns Vol. 1 **NEW!**	6 Tapes	$30.00
	Apostolic Patterns Vol. 2 **NEW!**	5 Tapes	$25.00
	Champions	5 Tapes	$25.00
	Angels	5 Tapes	$25.00
	Uncapping the Forces of God	5 Tapes	$25.00
	Power of Confidence	5 Tapes	$25.00
	Mystery of Godliness	5 Tapes	$25.00
	Retrofit	5 Tapes	$25.00
	Consecrated Heart	5 Tapes	$25.00
	Abolishing Death **NEW!**	4 Tapes	$20.00
	Miracle Seed Harvest	4 Tapes	$20.00
	Intimacy With God	4 Tapes	$20.00
	Perceptions Image	4 Tapes	$20.00
	The Intercession of Jesus	4 Tapes	$20.00
	Meditating on Supernatural	4 Tapes	$20.00
	Power of Obedience **NEW!**	4 Tapes	$20.00
	Ephesians Chapter One	4 Tapes	$20.00
	Fire is Your Future	4 Tapes	$20.00

Album Tape Sets   Buy Any 3 and Get 20% Off!

	Christ the Hope of Glory	4 Tapes	$20.00
	Unlimited Realm Vol. 1	4 Tapes	$20.00
	Weightiness of God	4 Tapes	$20.00
	Divine Capabilities	4 Tapes	$20.00
	Leading With Power	3 Tapes	$15.00
	The Order of Faith	3 Tapes	$15.00
	Glory of The Anointing	3 Tapes	$15.00
	Unlimited Realm Vol. 2	3 Tapes	$15.00
	Crucifixion of Empathy	3 Tapes	$15.00
	Purity -K. Hunter	3 Tapes	$15.00
	Breaking Selfishness	3 Tapes	$15.00
	Getting Dressed Power	3 Tapes	$15.00
	Prophetic Indicators	3 Tapes	$15.00
	Unlimited Finances	2 Tapes	$10.00
	Ephesians 3:17	2 Tapes	$10.00
	Vessels of Destiny	2 Tapes	$10.00
	Presenting A Yielded Will	2 Tapes	$10.00
	Power of Innocence	2 Tapes	$10.00
	Love Greatest Weapon	2 Tapes	$10.00
	Why People Get Sick?	2 Tapes	$10.00
	Ishmael & Isaac Miracle	2 Tapes	$10.00
	Men Maneuvered Devil	2 Tapes	$10.00
	Hiding in Christ -K. Hunter	2 Tapes	$10.00
	Confession Declares Position	2 Tapes	$10.00
	The Greatest Thing I Value **NEW!**	2 Tapes	$10.00

The Vision of Sword Ministries

The foundation of this ministry rests in Hebrews 4:12 which is summarized in the following statement, "Speaking the Truth in Revival, Piercing the Innermost Being." We are to remain carriers of revival, "Demonstrating Signs and Wonders, Decently and In Order, by the Power of the Holy Spirit."

Our vision is to see the stadiums of America and around the world filled to capacity in which the fullness of the Gospel of Christ, the Anointed One is declared unto salvation. Not just in persuasive words of man's wisdom, but in demonstration of the Spirit and in Power (Acts 2), which includes salvation according to Acts 10:44.

To see multitudes touched by the loving presentation of the power of God through power packed spirit filled books published in many different languages, world wide multi-media television and radio productions, and churches and Bible schools established in China and other nations, via Apostolic teams and multi-faceted Evangelistic operations.